VOLCANO DISASTERS

John Hawkins

FRANKLIN WATTS

This paperback edition published in 2014 by Franklin Watts

Franklin Watts
338 Euston Road
London NW1 3BH

Franklin Watts Australia
Level 17/207 Kent Street, Sydney NSW 2000

Produced by Arcturus Publishing Limited,
26/27 Bickels Yard, 151–153 Bermondsey Street, London SE1 3HA

Text: John Hawkins
Editors: Joe Harris
Design: Graham Rich
Cover design: Graham Rich

Picture credits:
Corbis: cover, 1, 10t, 10b, 11, 12, 14b, 19, 32, 35, 37, 38b, 44b, 45t, 45tc, 45bc, 45b, 47.
iStockphoto: 15. Getty: 16, 21, 22, 24b, 25, 26, 27, 28, 30b, 40, 44t, 44tc, 44c, 44bc.
Rex Features: 9. Science Photo Library: 4, 5, 6, 7, 8, 42, 43. Shutterstock: 14t, 18, 20, 24t, 30t, 34, 36, 38t.
Cover image: Reykjavik, Iceland. On the island of Heimaey, the Helgafjell Volcano continues its eruption on 27 January 1973. The eruption began four days earlier, on 23 January.

A CIP catalogue record for this book is available from the British Library.

Dewey Decimal Classification Number 363.3′495

ISBN 978 1 4451 3131 3

Printed in China

Franklin Watts is a division of Hachette Children's Books, an Hachette UK company.
www.hachette.co.uk

SL001930UK
Supplier 03, Date 0114, Print Run 3214

Contents

What Are Volcanoes?

A volcano is a hill or mountain on the earth's surface where magma – molten rock – erupts from deep beneath the ground. Above ground, the molten rock is known as lava. The peaks of volcanoes are made up of lava that has cooled and hardened after coming out of the ground, together with cinders and ash.

ERUPTIONS

Volcanic eruptions are among the most violent and spectacular natural events on earth. Accompanied by red-hot rivers of lava, towering clouds of ash and thick flows of mud, they can devastate the landscape and people's lives.

VOLCANOES AROUND THE WORLD

Volcanoes are found on land and under the sea. About 25 land volcanoes erupt every year. Some erupt with spectacular, huge explosions, but others erupt less violently. Some volcanoes erupt almost continuously, whereas others erupt only once every few hundred years.

Lava erupts from a volcano on the island of Bali in Indonesia.

This schoolbus, which became trapped in a lava flow in Hawaii, is now encased in rock.

VOLCANOES AND THE LANDSCAPE

Erupting volcanoes cover the landscape with lava, ash and mud. Over centuries, this creates mountains and islands. Much of the earth's surface is made up of rocks that have come from volcanoes. However, volcanoes can also be destructive. They can destroy plants and animal habitats, and kill thousands of people. Houses, villages and towns may be buried or burned.

 VULCAN, GOD OF THE FORGE

The word volcano comes from 'Vulcano', the name of an island off the coast of Italy. The ancient Romans believed that the god Vulcan lived in a volcano on the island, where he made weapons for the other gods, such as arrows, armour and lightning bolts. Fiery eruptions from the island's volcanoes were believed to be sparks from Vulcan's forge.

The Formation of Volcanoes

The solid ground beneath our feet is called the earth's crust. On land the crust is around 50 km (30 miles) thick, but beneath the oceans it is only about 5 km (3 miles) deep. Beneath the crust is another layer called the mantle, which is partly composed of molten rock, also known as magma. Volcanoes form in places where molten rock forces its way upward through the crust.

The giant cracks in this landscape in Iceland have been created by tectonic plates moving apart.

MOVING PLATES

The crust is made up of huge, slowly drifting pieces of rock called tectonic plates. These plates move across the mantle a couple of centimetres or so each year, pushed by currents in the hot rock below. Most volcanoes form along the plate boundaries, the lines where two plates meet.

The volcano of the Hawaiian Island of Oahu is fed by magma from below.

PLATES CRASHING TOGETHER

At boundaries, two plates are moving in different directions. They may push into each other or move apart. Where two plates collide, one may be forced to sink under the other. The plate melts as it dives into the mantle, making magma that rises again to produce volcanoes. These boundaries are called subduction zones or destructive boundaries.

PLATES PULLING APART

Places where plates move apart are called constructive boundaries. Magma rises up from the mantle to fill the gap between the plates. This is another cause of volcanic eruptions.

UNDERSEA VOLCANOES

Many more volcanoes are hidden under the oceans than can be seen on land. Most form along constructive boundaries on the ocean floor, where magma leaks out between tectonic plates that are moving apart. These boundaries are also called spreading ridges. The magma solidifies to make new crust on each side of the boundary. Other undersea volcanoes form at destructive boundaries.

Inside a Volcano

Deep beneath the visible part of a volcano – 100 km (60 miles) or more below – is a chamber full of magma. That chamber feeds into a hole called a vent, which reaches up to the earth's surface. At the top of a volcano there is often a dish-shaped hollow called a crater. During an eruption, magma rises from the magma chamber, through the vent, and out into the atmosphere.

Sugarloaf Mountain in Rio de Janeiro, Brazil, is made of hardened magma. The magma turned to rock in the vent of a volcano, before the volcano's cone eroded away.

COMPOSITE CONES

Most volcanoes on land are tall cones made up of layers of broken lava and ash. This type of volcano is called a composite cone or stratovolcano, and examples include Mount Fuji in Japan and Vesuvius in Italy. These volcanoes are giant heaps of loose rubble. Their layers were formed by many eruptions over thousands or even millions of years. A main vent leads to the centre and side vents lead to the volcano's lower slopes. Magma sometimes flows in between the layers of lava and ash and then solidifies, making the volcano more stable.

MAGMA

Magma is molten rock underground. Molten rock on the surface is called lava. Some types of magma are runny and flow easily, like syrup. Others are thick and sticky, like tar. Magma has a temperature of about 1,800 °F (980 °C).

RELEASE OF GAS

Magma also contains gas that is dissolved in it. When magma is deep inside the earth, high pressure keeps the gas dissolved. But when the magma rises through the vent of a volcano, the gas is released and bursts out of the volcano with the molten rock. This is what happens when you open a can of fizzy drink. Gas dissolved in the liquid bubbles out when you open the can, releasing the pressure.

Magma rises up the vent of a stratovolcano from the magma chamber deep underground. The volcano's layers are made up of material from previous eruptions.

ICELAND

Europe Is Grounded, 2010

Eyjafjallajoekull – which means 'island mountain glacier' – is not a major volcano in Icelandic terms. However, when it erupted in 2010 it had a direct impact on the lives of millions of people, as the volcanic ash plume spewing from Eyjafjallajoekull grounded planes across northern Europe for several weeks.

EVACUATION

After 200 years of lying dormant, Eyjafjallajoekull first erupted at 11.30 pm on 20 March 2010. The fissure opened directly across a popular hiking route. Fortunately, no one was in serious danger – the authorities had already evacuated about 600 people from the threatened area, around 120 km (75 miles) east of the capital, Reykjavik.

Ash billows from Eyjafjallajoekull on 21 April 2010.

THE SCIENCE OF PREDICTION

Scientists monitoring the volcano had detected hundreds of tiny earthquakes under the volcano starting in December 2009, together with a sudden expansion of the earth's crust. They were initially concerned that the eruption could cause a serious flood, as the centre of the volcano was located under a glacier. However, when this didn't happen, residents were allowed to return home after 24 hours.

Hikers watch lava pouring down the slopes of Eyjafjallajoekull.

FEARS

Nevertheless, the residents remained concerned about the possibility of further eruptions. Historically eruptions of Eyjafjallajoekull had been followed by eruptions of the nearby Katla, a far bigger and more dangerous volcano. An eruption of Katla would cause terrible flooding.

EYEWITNESS

Almost as soon as the initial evacuation was over, tourists began to pour into the area, keen to see the eruption taking place. Thousands of Icelanders made daytrips to see the eruption in progress. Tour operators offered visitors the opportunity to get up close to the volcano by snowmobile or helicopter.

A SECOND ERUPTION

On 14 April 2010, the volcano began to erupt again, this time from under a glacier. Melting waters from the glacier flooded into nearby rivers, and 800 people were evacuated. Meltwater poured into the volcanic vent, causing the eruption to become explosive. This resulted in ash being thrown miles up into the atmosphere.

The ash cloud pours into the air above Eyjafjallajoekull.

THE ASH CLOUD

Volcanic ash began to drift south and east from Iceland. Because there was not a lot of wind, the ash cloud remained very dense. The ash in the air posed a real danger to planes, since the ash could seriously damage their engines.

NO FLY ZONE

This resulted in the largest air traffic shutdown since World War II. Airspace was closed and flights were cancelled in countries including Denmark, Norway, Sweden, Finland, France, the UK and the Republic of Ireland. Between 15 and 23 April 2010, airspace over Northern Europe was shut down completely. Flights continued to be grounded in some countries right through to mid-May.

PUBLIC ANGER

Millions of people were stranded not just in Europe, but across the world. This led to a widespread anger among passengers, many of whom found themselves unable to return home. The aviation industry was hit hard: at the height of the crisis, it was losing £126 million every day.

WHY DID IT HAPPEN?

Ash is known to be dangerous to aircraft engines. If it gets into the engine of a plane, it blocks the ventilation holes that allow in cooling air, causing the engine to shut down. This is what happened to a British Airways flight in 1982 when it flew through the volcanic ash cloud of Mount Galunggung, Java, Indonesia. All four of its engines shut down – and it began to plummet to earth. Fortunately tragedy was averted as the pilot was able to restart three of the engines and land safely.

POMPEII

Trapped in Time: Pompeii, 79 CE

In 79 CE, the slopes of Mount Vesuvius, Italy, were covered with orchards, vineyards and olive groves. At the foot of the mountain lay the commercial and agricultural centre of Pompeii and the resort of Herculaneum. The inhabitants of this thriving city had no idea that Vesuvius was a dormant volcano.

HIDDEN THREAT

Vesuvius had not erupted within living memory. However, there were some telltale signs. The Greek geographer Strabo had remarked that Vesuvius was shaped like a volcano. There was also seismic activity in the area. An earthquake had destroyed Pompeii and Herculaneum 16 years before and they had had to be rebuilt.

Pompeii still stands today, a haunting reminder of the volcano's power.

Vesuvius looms over Pompeii, once a bustling commercial centre.

MYSTERIOUS CLOUD

On 24 August 79 CE, Gaius Plinius Secundus – better known as Pliny the Elder – was settling down for an afternoon's reading at his house at Misenum at the mouth of the Bay of Naples, when his sister asked him to come and have a look at a strange cloud. He climbed to the top of a nearby hill and saw a cloud rising from the mountains.

THUNDER AND FIRE

At around midday, Vesuvius had broken open with a sound like a thunderclap, shooting fire, ash and pumice 20 km (12 miles) into the sky. Realizing that he was witnessing a major event, Pliny the Elder ordered a ship to be made ready so that he could get a closer look.

ROOFS COLLAPSE

Vesuvius was pelting Pompeii with ash and pumice. Rocks as much as 20 cm (8 inches) across were falling from thousands of metres in the air, killing anyone they hit. The build-up of pumice caused roofs to collapse and the inhabitants fled.

EYEWITNESS

An account of what Pliny the Elder saw was recorded by his nephew, Pliny the Younger: 'The cloud was rising; watchers from our distance could not tell from which mountain, though later it was known to be Vesuvius. In appearance and shape it was like a tree – the umbrella pine would give the best idea of it. Like an immense tree trunk, it was projected into the air, and opened out with branches.'

DEADLY MISTAKE

After the initial eruption had died down, some Pompeiians returned to their city, thinking that the worst was over. Then a pyroclastic flow – a deadly mixture of ash, pumice and superheated steam – came surging down the mountain at 100 kph (over 60 mph).

ENCASED IN ASH

Most of the inhabitants were simply overcome where they stood. Their bodies were then covered with between 6 and 7 m (20 and 23 feet) of pumice and ash, keeping them perfectly preserved until excavation of the site began in the 19th century.

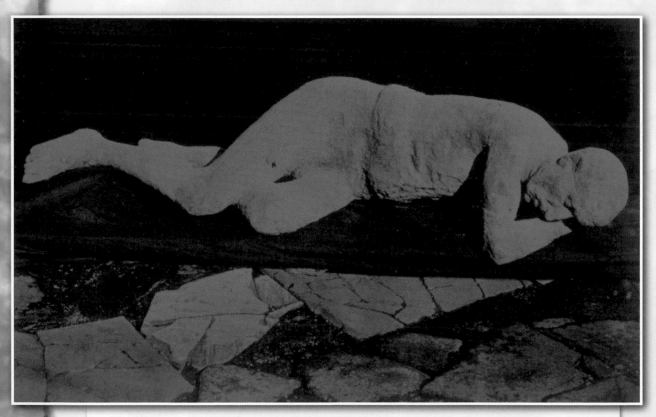

Many residents of Pompeii were covered with more than 6 m (20 feet) of pumice and ash, preserving them forever.

BOILING AVALANCHE

Herculaneum had escaped most of the first day's horrors. While 3.7 m (12 feet) of pumice and ash had landed on Pompeii, only 20 cm (8 inches) had fallen on Herculaneum. But then, without warning, the residents were hit by a surge of superheated steam that came rolling down the mountain. A boiling avalanche followed, smashing the buildings to pieces and searing everything in its path with temperatures of up to 500 °C (930 °F).

DEBRIS AND ROCK

An hour later another scalding cloud arrived, killing any survivors. In all, six surges hit the town, burying Herculaneum under 18 m (60 feet) of debris that turned into solid rock.

PRESERVED FOREVER

While the ash and pumice that covered Pompeii could be shovelled away, the rock that covered Herculaneum had to be removed with drills and chisels when the excavation began in 1980. Beneath it, as at Pompeii, there was a perfect time capsule. The people of Herculaneum had been preserved exactly as they were, going about their everyday business 19 centuries before.

 EYEWITNESS

By the evening of 24 August, Pliny the Elder had reached the fishing village of Stabiae, which was being shaken by violent tremors. He took a long bath before going to bed. The following morning he died. He had either been suffocated by sulphurous gas, or his weak heart had given out because of the difficulty he had experienced in breathing.

ICELAND

Skaptarjökul Splits Open, 1783

On 11 June 1783, the volcano Skaptarjökul, in Iceland, began to erupt. After a series of violent earthquakes, the sides of the mountain cracked and lava poured out. A stream of molten rock 60 m (nearly 200 feet) wide and up to 180 m (nearly 600 feet) deep filled a nearby gorge and overflowed, filling a lake and a complex of caves.

RIVER OF LAVA

There were further lava flows on 18 June and 3 August. The amount of ejected material was estimated to have had the same mass as Mont Blanc in France. At its peak, the mass of outpouring liquid rivalled the Amazon, the world's largest river.

CASUALTIES

The lava overwhelmed 20 villages. It is thought that more than 9,000 people were killed, out of a total Icelandic population of 50,000 at the time. Over 190,000 sheep, 28,000 horses and 11,000 head of cattle also died. This massive loss of life was caused by the toxic gas, streams of lava and floods caused by rivers blocked with lava.

FAMINE STRIKES

A famine was caused by the destruction of plant life and the loss of fish (a major part of the Icelandic diet) from coastal waters.

This is Skaptarjöekul seen from the air (in the foreground).

EYEWITNESS

Writing, in 1784, about the previous year's weather, Benjamin Franklin noted that the sunlight reaching the ground even hundreds of miles away had been diffused. A strange 'dry fog' had hung over the land and when the sun's rays 'were collected in the focus of a burning glass, they would scarcely kindle brown paper.' Franklin suggested that the 'vast quantities of smoke' emitted from Skaptarjökul had been responsible for this. The volcano Asama-yama in Japan also erupted in 1783, expelling quantites of ash and red-hot rocks. Together, the two volcanoes seem to have been the cause of the cooling Franklin noted.

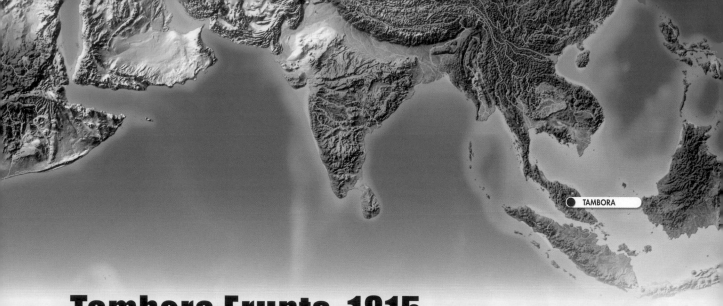

TAMBORA

Tambora Erupts, 1815

In 1815, the 4,000-m (13,000-foot) volcano Tambora, on the island of Sumbawa, near Java, erupted. The effects of this disaster were felt worldwide.

BACK TO LIFE

Since Europeans had first set foot in Indonesia, Tambora had been thought to be extinct. But in 1814 it began to emit small showers of ash. Then on the night of 5 April 1815 there was an earthquake.

DESTRUCTIVE BLASTS

The earthquake was followed by a series of explosive eruptions, some of which were heard 1,448 km (900 miles) away in Sumatra. The most violent eruption happened on the night of 11 to 12 April, and the explosions continued until July. In all, more than 150 cubic km (36 cubic miles) of solid material were blasted into the air, leaving the mountain a mile shorter than before.

RAINING ROCKS

Ash and smoke darkened the sky for nearly 500 km (over 300 miles) around, even at midday. Rocks the size of human heads fell in the nearby area and ash fell up to 1,300 km (over 800 miles) away.

Every part of Javanese society was affected by the eruption of the nearby volcano.

HUMAN IMPACT

Subsidence (sinking land) left a nearby village, also called Tambora, submerged under 5.5 m (18 feet) of water. Some 12,000 people died in the eruption. A further 80,000 died of starvation and disease caused by the devastation of the area.

EARTHQUAKE

The collapse of the volcanic crater caused an earthquake that was felt more than 480 km (nearly 300 miles) away. Another quake shook Sumbawa on 13 January 1909. Around that time lava began to flow from a cone that had formed in the crater in 1847.

EYEWITNESS

Sir Stamford Raffles, founder of the British colony of Singapore, was serving as military governor of Java when Tambora erupted. He reported that the sky was dark at noon and falling ash covered the island. Glowing lava could be seen on top of the cone and he heard what sounded like the sound of artillery fire or distant thunder.

Mount Tambora is still an active volcano, although it has not erupted since 1967.

ASH CLOUDS

The effects of the 1815 Tambora eruption were felt around the world. Much of the material ejected from the volcano was in the form of fine ash, which was blasted into the atmosphere.

THE YEAR WITHOUT A SUMMER

There was so much ash that the amount of sunlight falling on the earth was cut significantly. This caused a dramatic drop in temperature across the globe and 1816 became known as 'the year without a summer'.

SNOW AND STARVATION

Snow fell in New England in July. Although the US was able to feed itself – its warmer, southern farms were able to meet the shortfall – there was famine in Canada. In some parts of Northern Europe, people were reduced to eating rats.

THE LONGEST WINTER

In Switzerland, grain prices rose 300 per cent. France was particularly hard hit because the crop failures there came soon after the devastation of the Napoleonic Wars. Farmers who dared to take their produce to market needed armed escorts to prevent them being attacked and robbed by starving mobs along the way.

COLD SPELLS

Some scientists argue that the catastrophic summer of 1816 was not necessarily tied to the eruption of Tambora. This is because it fell within the normal range of climate change. However, similar cold spells have been seen after other major eruptions. After the eruption of Krakatoa in 1884, the amount of sunlight falling on the earth was 16 per cent less than previous years and 12 per cent below the norm. It dropped by 4 per cent after Alaska's Bogoslov and several other volcanoes erupted in 1889. A drop of 13 per cent was recorded after the eruption of Mount Pelée and La Soufrière in 1902.

City of the Dead, St Pierre, 1902

In April 1902, St Pierre in Martinique was a thriving town of 30,000 people. It had a cathedral, a military hospital, cafés, dancehalls and a theatre. On sunny days, the local people would picnic on the slopes of nearby Mount Pelée and swim in the clear waters of the lake on its peak. They had no idea that a terrible disaster was about to befall them.

FIRST WARNING

The French colonized the Caribbean island of Martinique in 1635 and built its commercial capital, St Pierre, at the foot of a seemingly extinct volcano – Mount Pelée. However, in 1792 the volcano began to rumble and a sprinkling of ash dusted the upper slopes.

St Pierre was a town of 30,000 people, established at the base of Mount Pelée.

ANOTHER WARNING

In 1851, the volcano rumbled again, this time dusting the prosperous suburbs of St Pierre with ash. However, when the rain came and washed the ash away, everyone forgot about the volcano.

ROCKS AND CINDERS

In April 1902, the mountain began to rumble again, and a vent around the summit began to belch sulphurous gases. On 23 April, there were tremors and a light rain of cinders fell on the southern and western slopes. Then on 25 April the mountain began to blast rock and ash high into the sky.

SMOKE AND LIGHTNING

At 11.30 pm on the night of 2 May, there was a massive explosion. The pillar of black smoke that climbed from the summit was surrounded by lightning. In the morning, the people found their city undamaged, but covered once more in a light dusting of white ash, like a fresh fall of snow.

Mount Pelée erupts and the devastation begins.

ASH CLOUD

By 4 May, the cloud of ash was so dense that ships were afraid to sail through it. The sea bobbed with dead birds and a number of peasant children from outlying regions were seen wandering around the city in a daze. The following day, the electrical disturbances around the summit were so intense that they knocked out the power in the city. More peasants poured into the city from outlying regions, bringing their livestock. Some local people began to flee to nearby Guadeloupe.

TOURISTS

On the morning of 7 May, the passenger ship *Roraima* dropped anchor in the harbour and another steamer, the *Roddam*, moored close inshore so the passengers could view the volcano.

CUT OFF

It was Ascension Day and, that evening while the people of St Pierre were at church, the telegraph operator at the post office began sending his daily report to the capital Fort-de-France, 18 km (11 miles) away. At 7.52 pm, the telegraph line went dead and Fort-de-France was plunged into darkness.

The devastation in St Pierre was total.

St Pierre became a sea of rubble.

ONCOMING CLOUD

The crew of the *Pouyer-Quertier*, a repair ship 13 km (8 miles) offshore, saw the side of Mount Pelée open. A huge black cloud shot out horizontally, while a mushroom cloud curled up into the sky. The horizontal cloud rolled noiselessly down the slope towards St Pierre, clinging to the ground.

CITY IN FLAMES

Inside the cloud there was a bright, fiery glow and flashes of lightning. When the cloud swallowed the city, everything it touched burst into flames. On the docks, a thousand barrels of rum exploded in a huge roar. On board the *Pouyer-Quertier*, the crew could feel the heat. Red-hot rocks rained down on her decks.

EYEWITNESS

Further out to sea, the Comte de Fitz-James, with his travelling companion Baron de Fontenilliat, watched the destruction of St Pierre. He wrote: 'From a boat in the roadstead, I witnessed the cataclysm that came upon the city.... From the depths of the earth came rumblings, an awful music which cannot be described. I called my companion's name, and my voice echoed back at me from a score of angles. All the air was filled with the acrid vapors that had belched from the mouth of the volcano....

'We saw the cable ship *Grappler* keel over in the whirlwind, and sink as through drawn down... by some force from below.'

CITY OF THE DEAD

In the wake of the eruption, the whole population of St Pierre – some 30,000 people – died. Superheated steam with temperatures of over 1,000 °C (1,830 °F), mixed with lethal gas and red-hot ash. This created a deadly pyroclastic flow – a river of hot ash and rock.

The effects of the erupting Mount Pelée were horrifying.

TERRIBLE SUFFERING

People's clothing had been ripped from them as if they had been hit by a cyclone. Some were burned beyond recognition; others appeared untouched. Some seem to have died suddenly, with no time to react; others suffered horribly.

A SINGLE SURVIVOR

Extraordinarily, there was a survivor. He was a convicted murderer named Ludger Sylbaris, who had been locked in an underground cell. He said hot, dark air mixed with ash had come through the bars, burning his flesh. He cried out in agony, but no one came to help him.

FREEDOM

For four days, he remained locked in his cell, knowing nothing of the fate of the city. The salvage workers heard his moans and dug him out. Mount Pelée had let him live, and the authorities decided to give him his freedom. He later toured with the famous Barnum and Bailey circus.

AFTERMATH

St Pierre burned for days and it took weeks to bury the dead. In October a lava dome began to form, raising the height of Mount Pelée by about 300 m (nearly 1,000 feet). The city never recovered. It was rebuilt on a much smaller scale. Mount Pelée erupted again in 1929, but this time St Pierre was evacuated.

EYEWITNESS

On 8 May 1902, the governor of Martinique sent a warship to find out what had happened to St Pierre. The Comte de Fitz-James followed its landing party ashore. Entering a strange, alien landscape, they found no one.

'We saw great stones that seemed to be marvels of strength, but when touched with the toe of a boot they crumbled into impalpable dust. I picked up an iron bar…. The fire that came down from Mount Pelée had taken from the iron all of its strength. When I twisted it, it fell into filaments, like so much broom straw….'

The Destruction of Armero, 1985

Colombia's tallest volcano, Nevado del Ruiz, exploded violently at 3.06 pm on 13 November 1985. This came in the wake of 51 weeks of minor earthquakes and spouts of steam erupting from the volcano.

The Red Cross evacuated Armero when Nevado del Ruiz first erupted. The organization later played a vital part in the aftermath of the disaster.

ARMERO IN DANGER

Two hours later pumice fragments and ash were showering down on the town of Armero. The mayor went on the radio and assured citizens that there was no danger. But at 7 pm the Red Cross ordered an evacuation of the town. Shortly afterwards, however, the ash stopped falling. The evacuation was called off and calm was restored.

HIDDEN THREAT

Another two hours later, molten rock began to erupt from the summit crater and melt the mountain's snow cap. But storm clouds obscured the summit area and no one below could see what was going on.

DEADLY LAHARS

Meltwater mixed with ash creating hot 'lahars' – or volcanic mudflows. One flowed down the gorge of the River Cauca and engulfed the village of Chinchina, killing 1,927 people. Another, travelling at over 50 kph (over 30 mph), burst through a dam on the River Lagunillas and arrived at Armero at 11 pm. Most of the town was swept away or buried in only a few short minutes, killing most of the townspeople.

EYEWITNESS

Colombian geology student José Luis Restrepo was in Armero when the lahar hit in 1985. 'The electric power went out. That's when we started hearing noises that sounded like something toppling…. When we went out, the cars were swaying and running people down. There was total darkness. The only light was provided by car headlights. We were running and were about to reach the corner when a river of water came down the streets. We turned around screaming and ran back toward the hotel.'

A NIGHTMARISH SCENE

When rescuers arrived at Armero the following day, they found a tangle of trees, cars and dead bodies scattered throughout an ocean of grey mud. Injured survivors lay moaning in agony while rescue workers struggled frantically to save them.

DISASTER AREA

In all, some 23,000 people and 15,000 animals were killed. Another 4,500 people were injured and some 8,000 people were made homeless. The estimated cost of the disaster was US $1 billion, or about one fifth of the Colombia's Gross National Product.

WARNING SIGNS

The tragedy could have been averted. Nevado del Ruiz had been giving warning signs in the form of minor earthquakes and steam jets for nearly a year. A scientific commission had visited the crater in late February and a report of the volcanic activity appeared in the newspaper *La Patria* in early March.

MUDFLOWS PREDICTED

By July, seismologists in various other countries had plotted the magma rising under the volcano. A UN-funded report concluded that even with a moderate eruption there was 'a hundred percent probability of mudflows... with great danger for Armero, Ambalema, and the lower part of the River Chinchina'.

DANGER IGNORED

The UN report was published six weeks before the disaster, but only ten copies were circulated. Government officials dismissed the report as 'too alarming' and refused to evacuate people.

More than 23,000 people were killed in Armero when lahars swept down from the erupting Nevado del Ruiz volcano.

EYEWITNESS

Geology student José Luis Restrepo continues his story: 'The waters were dragging beds along, overturning cars, sweeping people away. We went back to the hotel.... Suddenly, I heard bangs, and looking toward the rear of the hotel I saw something like foam, coming down out of the darkness. It was a wall of mud. It crashed into the rear of the hotel, smashing the walls. Then the ceiling slab fractured. The entire building was destroyed and smashed to pieces.... I covered my face, thinking I was going to die horribly.'

Mount Pinatubo, Philippines, 1991

Prior to 1991, Mount Pinatubo, on the Philippine island of Luzon, was a relatively unknown volcano. It lay dormant for 40,000 years until 2 April 1991. However, its 1991 eruption was one of the largest of the 20th century.

FIRST ERUPTION

The initial eruption of Pinatubo devastated 0.65 square km (quarter of a square mile) of forested land. It stripped vegetation over a larger area, and carried ash 13 km (8 miles) away. There were no injuries or deaths that time, but some 2,000 people were evacuated.

ANOTHER BLAST

Seismic (earthquake) activity continued from April to mid-May. On 12 June, 12 hours of tremors and minor explosions were followed by a major volcanic blast. The blast threw ash and rocks 24 km (15 miles) into the air. Debris fell up to 20 km (12 miles) away.

A truck drives away from an ash cloud after an eruption on Mount Pinatubo.

WATCHING THE COLLAPSE

Infrared monitors from the nearby US Air Force base were used to monitor the volcano as it collapsed in on itself, leaving the summit some 137 m (450 feet) lower than before. Further explosions razed all vegetation within a 1.6 km (1 mile) radius of the crater and trees up to 8 km (5 miles) away lost all their foliage.

CONTINUING ERUPTIONS

Between 14 and 16 June, the explosions continued, mixing ash and volcanic debris with the heavy rain from the typhoons that had also hit the area. Rain falling into the crater lake caused secondary explosions. Vast swathes of farmland and fish farms were destroyed and 650,000 people were put out of work. Further eruptions continued until 1995.

Soufrière Hills, Montserrat, 1997

Since British settlers arrived on the island in 1632, Montserrat had been considered a paradise. But in 1997 a long-dormant volcano turned the island into a living hell. Apart from the northern tip of the island, Montserrat became a nightmare of molten lava, ash clouds, noxious gases and rock falls.

THE BEGINNING

With no recorded historical eruptions of the volcano on Montserrat, it was thought to be so harmless that it was known only as the Soufrière Hills. But, on 18 July 1995, it began to erupt. As lava flowed towards outlying farms, people had to be evacuated. After this eruption, the volcano was continuously monitored. However, it was still considered to be relatively safe.

PLYMOUTH IS ENGULFED

A second, much more violent eruption happened on 25 June 1997. This time the volcano claimed the lives of 33 people. Only ten of their bodies were recovered. The island's capital, Plymouth, was covered with ash. As lava flows reached Plymouth's outskirts, buildings burst into flames and fire tore through the town.

Plymouth, the abandoned capital of Montserrat, is covered in ash.

EVACUATION

By 25 August, only 4,000 of the island's original 11,000 inhabitants remained. The rest had been evacuated to Britain or other Caribbean islands. After so much destruction, there was little reason for them to stay behind.

AID

Those who fled received £2,500 compensation from the British government. Those who stayed were given aid. Pop artists including Paul McCartney and Elton John staged a benefit concert in London for the people of Montserrat.

LEARNING FROM DISASTERS

The inhabitants should have known about the danger. Seismic activity in the form of earthquakes had been recorded and volcanic vents had occasionally belched out sulphurous gases from the magma under the Soufrière Hills. Soufrière in French means 'sulphur mine'.

La Soufrière, St Vincent, 1902

Montserrat is not the only island in the Caribbean to have an active volcano named 'Soufrière' – La Soufrière on the island of St Vincent erupted in 1902.

This image shows an aerial view of a volcano crater on the island of St Vincent.

BOILING LAKE

The eruption began with a series of earthquakes in April. In May, puffs of steam began to emerge from the peak. On 4 May, the heat on the island became unusually oppressive. People found they could barely breathe. On 5 May, the lake in the volcanic crater began to boil.

YELLOW FLAMES

Two days later, a dark column of smoke rose from the top of the cone, reaching far up into the heavens. The mouth of the crater itself glowed like a gigantic forge belching a huge jet of yellow flames. The mass of smoke spread out into streams extending for miles, and clouds of sulphurous vapour flowed out from the bowl of the crater and began to roll down the mountain slopes.

SUPERHEATED

A pyroclastic flow – a mixture of superheated gases and ash – rolled down the mountain killing 1,680 people, although it is said that hundreds escaped death by hiding in a rum cellar. Most of the island's remaining population of indigenous Carib people were wiped out.

 EYEWITNESS

A fisherman told of his lucky escape: 'I was fishing at some distance from the shore when my boatman said to me, "Look at the Soufrière, sir. It's smoking." We reached shore and started to run for our lives. We were soon enveloped in impenetrable darkness and I was unable to distinguish the white shirt of my boatman at a yard's distance. But as he knew every inch of the ground, I held on to a stick he had, and so we stumbled on until we reached a place of safety... At last we emerged from the pall of death, half suffocated, and with our temples throbbing as if they were going to burst.'

RIVERS OF LAVA

More earthquakes followed and six separate streams of lava began pouring down the mountainside. At night the eruption was visible from St Lucia, 80 km (50 miles) away.

Richmond Great House was destroyed and buried in volcanic ash following the eruption of Soufrière, on 8 May 1902.

BLACK COLUMN

By 8 May, a column of black smoke had risen to a height of 13 km (8 miles). There was loud thunder and spectacular lightning, while the mountain 'groaned under the weight of accumulated fury'. Rocks and ash fell for miles around. The island was plunged into darkness.

ASH FROM THE SKY

A black rain began to fall and the air was heavy with the smell of sulphur. A steamer on its way to the largest town, Kingstown, encountered floating ash and pumice, and a cloud of sulphurous gas. When it reached Kingstown – about 13 km (8 miles) from the crater – it found the streets 5 cm (2 inches) deep in rock and ash.

LIGHTNING STRIKES

Among the survivors were many who had been struck by lightning and were paralysed, or who had been scorched and blistered by the hot sand. By 9 May, the showers of rock had stopped but the lava continued to flow. In all, nearly a third of the island had been devastated and 213 m (700 feet) had been lost from the top of the mountain. Hundreds of bodies lay unburied. In one ravine alone, 87 corpses were found. They were covered with quicklime to prevent the spread of disease.

 EYEWITNESS

One survivor had been rescued with others from a collapsed house. 'We heard the mountain roaring the whole morning,' he said. 'We did not like to abandon our homes, so we chanced it.... The big explosion must have taken place at half-past two o'clock. There was fire all around me, and I could not breathe. My hands and feet got burned, but I managed to reach the house where the others were. In two hours, everything was over.... My burns got so painful and stiff that I could not move. We remained until Sunday morning without food or water. Five persons died, and as none of us could throw the bodies out, or even move, we had to lie alongside the bodies until we were rescued.'

Looking to the Future

Vulcanologists are scientists who study volcanic activity. They investigate what happens to volcanoes before they erupt and while they are erupting. These investigations help the scientists to understand how volcanoes work. They also help them to predict when a volcano will erupt so that people can be evacuated.

TAKING MEASUREMENTS

Every eruption is different. Vulcanologists examine lava flows, layers of ash, mudflows and the volcanic rock around volcanoes. They measure the thickness of different layers of material and how old the layers are.

A vulcanologist uses a long probe to measure the temperature of molten lava. His shiny protective suit reflects some of the intense heat.

HAZARD MAPS

Vulcanologists' measurements tell them how often a volcano has erupted, and how violent each eruption was. With this information about a volcano's history, vulcanologists are able to draw up hazard maps. These maps show which areas around the volcano are likely to be hit by future eruptions.

PREDICTING ERUPTIONS

Vulcanologists also take measurements to see whether a volcano is likely to erupt soon. The measurements show if magma deep underground is beginning to move. For example, the scientists take samples of gas coming from the volcano's vent. If it contains a gas called sulphur dioxide, then magma is probably rising upward. Measuring devices called seismometers are used to detect earthquakes.

The different colours in this image of Stromboli, Italy, show the ground temperature of different parts of the island. Red areas are recent lava flows giving out heat.

MOUNT PINATUBO

In 1991, vulcanologists successfully predicted the violent eruption of Mount Pinatubo. Their seismometers had detected hundreds of small earthquakes, and gas samples had shown an increase in sulphur dioxide. Danger areas around the volcano were evacuated, and the lives of tens of thousands of people were saved.

Timeline

24 August 79 CE, Pompeii, Italy
Mount Vesuvius erupted, firing ash and pumice 20 km (12 miles) into the sky. The initial eruption was followed by a deadly pyroclastic flow that covered Pompeii, killing its inhabitants but preserving the city just as it was that day.

11 June 1783, Iceland
Violent earthquakes triggered an eruption of Skaptarjökul, a volcano in Iceland. The mountain cracked and rivers of lava started to spill out, killing an estimated 9,000 people.

April 1815, Java, Indonesia
A series of explosive eruptions from Java's Tambora volcano blasted huge amounts of rock, ash and smoke into the air, darkening the sky for 480 km (nearly 300 miles) around. Some 12,000 people died, followed by a further 80,000 from starvation and disease.

2 May 1902, St Pierre, Martinique, Caribbean
Ignoring earlier warning signs, many residents of St Pierre were at church when the side of Mount Pelée opened and a huge cloud rolled down the slope enveloping the city and killing some 30,000 people.

May 1902, St Vincent, Caribbean
Earthquakes and a build-up of volcanic activity in the innocently named La Soufrière on this Caribbean island forced a pillar of dense smoke into the air and a pyroclastic flow down the mountain, killing 1,680 people.

13 November 1985, Armero, Colombia

Despite warnings and calls for evacuation, 23,000 people were killed when Colombia's tallest volcano, Nevado del Ruiz, exploded violently. It sent lahars in different directions; one sweeping away the town of Armero.

April–June 1991, Luzon, Philippines

Dormant for 40,000 years, Mount Pinatubo on the Philippine island of Luzon first erupted on 2 April with no loss of life. On 12 June, it erupted in one of the largest explosions of the 20th century, spreading debris for up to 20 km (12 miles). Many were evacuated but hundreds still died.

25 June 1997, Plymouth, Montserrat

The long-dormant Soufrière Hills turned this paradise island into a living hell. It first erupted on 18 July 1995, but it was the second eruption that covered the city with ash and lava flows, setting the town alight and displacing thousands. In all, 33 people lost their lives.

March and April 2010, Iceland

When the small volcano of Eyjafjallajoekull initally erupted on 20 March, no one was hurt and people even went to watch. A second eruption on 14 April sent a cloud of ash miles up into the air, resulting in the largest air traffic shutdown since World War II. Thousands of travellers around the world were stranded for weeks.

Glossary

ash powder made up of tiny pieces of glassy rock

ash cloud a large cloud of ash blown into the air by a volcano. This is also called an eruption column.

boundary the place where the edges of two tectonic plates meet

cinders small pieces of red or black rock filled with gas bubbles

composite cone a steep-sided volcano that is made up of layers of ash and lava

constructive boundary a boundary where two tectonic plates move away from each other and new rock forms in the gap that is made

crater a bowl-shaped hole in the top of a volcano

crust the solid, outer layer of the earth

destructive boundary boundary where two tectonic plates collide, forcing one to sink into the earth beneath the other and melt

diffuse to spread out over a wide area

forge the place where a blacksmith works, bending and hammering red-hot iron into objects

glacier a slow-moving river of ice that flows down a valley in high mountain ranges

indigenous native to a particular place

lava molten or solid rock on the earth's surface that has come from a volcano

magma molten rock deep under the earth's surface

magma chamber a magma-filled space deep under a volcano

mudflow a fast-moving mixture of ash and water. Also called a lahar.

pumice a light volcanic rock that is full of holes, like a sponge

pyroclastic flow a thick cloud of red-hot ash and rock that flows down the side of a volcano

quicklime a white rocky material that burns flesh

seismic to do with earthquakes, or the movement of the earth

seismometer a device that measures tiny vibrations in the ground

tectonic plate one of the giant pieces that make up the earth's crust

vent a hole through the middle of a volcano from which ash and lava escape

Further Information

FURTHER READING

100 Facts: Volcanoes, by Chris Oxlade (Miles Kelly, 2009)

Graphic Natural Disasters: Volcanoes, by Rob Shone (Franklin Watts, 2010)

My Best Book of Volcanoes, by Simon Adams (Kingfisher Books, 2007)

Volcano! The Icelandic Eruption of 2010 and Other Hot, Smoky, Fierce, and Fiery Mountains, by Judy and Dennis Fradin (National Geographic Kids, 2010)

Volcanoes, by Anne Schreiber (National Geographic Kids, 2008).

WEBSITES

National Geographic
www.nationalgeographic.com/forcesofnature/interactive/index.html

Volcano Stories and Photos
www.volcanoes.com

Weather Information
www.weatherwizkids.com/weather-volcano.htm

Index